## Praise for *How to Have Fun Without Failing Out*

*"How to Have Fun Without Failing Out* can literally save your college life. The wisdom that Rob Gilbert provides in this book is invaluable for any college student."
**—Kenneth Blanchard, Ph.D.**
Coauthor of *The One Minute Manager*

"Urgent memo to every college student in America: READ THIS BOOK . . . BEFORE IT'S TOO LATE."
**—Sarah Hamilton**
Former Director of New Student Programs,
University of Massachusetts Amherst

"If you're attending college—read this book before you attend another class. If you're paying for someone to attend college—buy this book AND MAKE SURE THAT PERSON READS IT!"
**—Dr. Kirk Peters**
Dean of Student Affairs, Tunxis Community College, CT

"I highly recommend *How to Have Fun Without Failing Out*. Read it. Read it again. Pick out between three and five items and do them every day, and you can't help but be successful."
**—Dr. Nate Zinsser**
Author of *Dear Dr. Psych*

*"How to Have Fun Without Failing Out* is great. Every college student should have a copy. There is wisdom here, easily digested in less than half an hour, that takes most of us a lifetime to learn."
**—Robert W. Bly**
Author of *The Elements of Business Writing*
and *The Elements of Technical Writing*

"Uncommo  l to any freshman's
survival."

**—Dr. Elliot Engel**
lina State University

"Powerful, inspiring, and just what you need to leap ahead—in college or anywhere else! I love this! Open any page, read any tip, and your life can change."

**—Dr. Joe Vitale**
Author of *Life's Missing Instruction Manual*

"I love your 430 secrets. I plan to share it with our faculty who teach our introduction to college course."

**—Dr. Joann La Perla-Morales**
President, Middlesex County College, NJ

"FANTASTIC! Finally a book that shows students just what it takes to succeed in college. *How to Have Fun Without Failing Out* is funny, inspirational, thought provoking, and most important, these ideas really work. . . . Follow the sage advice offered by Dr. Gilbert, and you will succeed."

**—Jeffrey Keller**
President, Attitude Is Everything

"Dr. Gilbert has mined a lifetime of experience to create these nuggets of golden wisdom. SIMPLY GREAT!"

**—Bryan Mattimore**
Author of *99% Inspiration*

"Everything you need to know to have a successful college career and life can be found in this wisdom-packed collection of thoughts and ideas. Rob Gilbert has done a superb job of developing a road map for success for college students. I wish I had read it when I was in college."

**—Diane Tracy**
Author of *Take This Job and Love It*

# HOW TO HAVE FUN

## WITHOUT

# FAILING OUT

## 430 Tips from a College Professor

### ROB GILBERT, PH.D.

Health Communications, Inc.
Deerfield Beach, Florida

*www.hcibooks.com*

**Library of Congress Cataloging-in-Publication Data**

Gilbert, Rob, Ph.D.

How to have fun without failing out : 430 tips from a college
professor / Rob Gilbert.

    p. cm.

    ISBN-13: 978-0-7573-0577-1 (trade paper)

    ISBN-10: 0-7573-0577-6 (trade paper)

    1. College students—Life skills guides. 2. College student
orientation. I. Title.

LB2343.3.G55 2007

378.1'98—dc22

                                    2006103118

HCI, its logos and marks are trademarks of Health Communications, Inc.

Publisher: Health Communications, Inc.
              3201 S.W. 15th Street
              Deerfield Beach, FL 33442–8190

*Interior book design and formatting by Dawn Von Strolley Grove*

*This book is dedicated to my mother,*
*Corinne Ellis Gilbert, who said,*
*"I wish my son had read this before he went to college.*
*It would have saved all of us a lot of headaches."*

*This book is also dedicated to*
*Sue Burghard Brooks,*
*whose insights, ideas, and brilliance have*
*added so much to every page!*

# CONTENTS

# ACKNOWLEDGMENTS

"I not only use all of the brains I have, but all of the brains I can borrow."
—Woodrow Wilson, the 28th president of the United States

During my undergraduate years at the University of Massachusetts Amherst, I learned that it's not fun to have *too much* fun. During grad school at UMass, I learned that it's possible to work hard *and* have fun. At Montclair State University, I learned that when you're doing what you love, work is the most fun of all.

■　■　■

I'd like to thank the following people, who, whether they realize it or not, helped me write this book:

Rob Ades, Ed Agresta, Rachel Amos, Dr. Ree Arnold, Amy Asmuth, Coach Homer Barr, Coach Evan Baumgartner, Art Bell, Yogi Berra, Robert Bly, Dr. Wayne Bond, Joan Braner, Sue Brooks, Wayne Burns, Dr. Kimberly Bush, Eric Butterworth, Michele Campagna, Dale Carnegie, Larry Cecchini, Laura Chartrand, Sandy Choron, Angelo Colon, Doug Cooney, Dr. Linda Cozzens, Dr. Linda Crescione, Pat Cuntrera, Melissa Curtin, Dr. Richard Damon, Jr., John Davis, Dr. Donna Dennis, Dr. Dominica Desiderioscioli, Matt DiMaio, Dawn Marie Dowd, George and Sarah Ellis, Marion and Dr. Sydney Ellis, Ed Ferraro, Frank Fillipelli, Dr. Michele Fisher, Irene Frankel, Estelle Frese, Ann Geissler, Coach Oliver

Gelston, Dr. Nancy Giardina, Corinne and Philmore M. Gilbert, Jay Gittleson, Andrea Gold, Dr. Alan Goldberg, Jonah Goldstein, Dr. Marsha Grant-Ford, Dr. Lise Greene, Pete Greider, Dr. Klara Gubacs-Collins, Ray Guidetti, Lisa Gulisano, Phil Hall, Sarah Hamilton, Dr. Paul Hartunian, Paul Harvey, Lorraine Hashian, Angel Herbert, Michael Heslep, James Hester, Dr. George Horn and Dr. Joan Schleede-Horn, Dr. Robert Horn, Dr. Robert James, Cornelius Jameson, Jill Jeffrey, Coach Chuck Johnson, Russell Jones, Dr. Susana Juniu, Elliott Kalb, Dr. Gary Kamen, Dr. Bill Kane, Dave Kaplan, Lee Kemp, Frank Kendra, Dr. Walter Kroll, Leslie Laing, Dr. Jeffrey Lant, Harry Lorrayne, Dr. Leonard Lucenko, Mary Lyman, Christine Marie, Dr. Carolyn Masterson, Linda Maxwell, Coach John McCarthy, Dr. Felicia McGinty, Melissa Merced, Dr. David Middlemas, Professor Ed Mills, Vin Mitchell, Coach Mark Monteyne, Ray Napolitano, George Noory, Amy Olson, Janice Pedicino, Dr. Kirk Peters, Tom Peters, Dr. Dorene Petrosky, Peter Petrovic, Arlene Pomar, Gary Pritchard, Joyce Restaino, Coach Steve Rome, Steven Rosa, Paula and Dr. Ray Rosenstock, Laura Ryblewski, Eduardo Saavedra, Kathy Sadowsky, Melissa Sapio, Dr. Susan Schwager, Dr. Nathan Schwartz-Salant, Brenda Sheehan, John Sikes, Jr, Ed Smith, Frank Somma, Mary Spellicy, Geoff Stec, Dr. Bill Sullivan, Patty Sullivan, Professor Tim Sullivan, Natalie and John Surie, Dr. Richard Taubald, Professor Tete Tetens, Dr. Richard Tobin, Dr. Joseph Toth, Coach Mike Tully, Grace Tung, Darren Ventre, Bill Walsh, Dan "Bull" Walsh, Bogna Wawrzeniuk, George Wood, Karen Wydra, and Dan Zadra.

# Rob Gilbert, Ph.D.

**From:**      Rob Gilbert, Ph.D.

**To:**         Students

**Subject:**   How to have fun without failing out

In September 1964, I began my freshman year at the University of Massachusetts Amherst. It's now the twenty-first century, and I'm a professor at Montclair State University in New Jersey.

I've spent the last forty-two years in college—first as a student, then as a staff member, and now as a professor. What I've discovered is that most colleges and universities offer courses on just about everything except how to excel in college. That's why I wrote this book—to help you excel. *How to Have Fun Without Failing Out* is your own personal course on college success.

It took me more than forty years to gain the insights and develop the strategies necessary to write this book. I wish I had it in my hands back in 1964, and I hope my hindsight will become your foresight.

# INTRODUCTION

## Before We Get Started . . .

All the college students I've ever met have two things in common:

1. They want to graduate and get their diplomas.
2. They want to have a great time while in college.

I speak at colleges and universities all over the country. I usually begin by asking the audience, "How many of you are *in* school this semester?"

Every single person shoots a hand into the air.

Then I ask, "How many of you are *into* school?"

Only a few cautiously raise their hands. The rest of them look at me quizzically.

Then I explain, "Colleges don't need any more people who just show up—they need more *students*. There's a huge difference between *going to school* and *being a student*. If you're *in* school, you're merely going to class. If you're *into* school, you're a student. If you're *in* school—you're enrolled. If you're *into* school—you're involved."

This book is about being *into it*—both in and out of the classroom.

One of the most "into-it" students I've ever taught was Melissa Sapio. She graduated from Montclair State University in May 2001 with a degree in psychology and a perfect 4.0 GPA.

Every semester Melissa returns to campus and speaks in my classes. First, she reviews her strategies for academic success with the students. (In fact, I've included many of her strategies in this book!) Then she answers questions. My students always ask her things like:

"Did you have a *boyfriend* when you were in school?"
"Were you involved in any campus *activities*?"
"Did you have a *job*?"

Basically, my students want to know if Melissa had a life or if she was just a grade-getting machine. They also want to know if she ever partied or if she spent every single waking moment in the library. The students are usually surprised by her answers.

Melissa *did* have a boyfriend, she *was* involved in extracurricular activities, and she *had* a job . . . and she got all As! It's true: Melissa had a great time in college, and SHE GOT ALL As!

She studied *and* she partied. She did it *all* while she was in college, and YOU CAN TOO! Let's get started. . . .

# Chapter 1

---

**From:**      Rob Gilbert, Ph.D.

**To:**        Students

**Subject:**   Get Motivated!



Action may not always bring happiness,
but there is no happiness without
action.

> —Benjamin Disraeli,
> British prime minister (1868, 1874–1880)

---

# The Ten Commandments of College Success

1. Show up.

2. Pay attention.

3. Ask questions.

4. Ask for help.

5. Help others.

6. Take notes.

7. Do the work.

8. Do not cheat.

9. No matter what, don't quit.

10. Graduate, then celebrate!

# Dr. Gilbert's Two Guarantees

**GUARANTEE #1:**
College will not be easy.

**GUARANTEE #2:**
College will be worth it!

## Recognizing Your Purpose

### Tip #1

What's your compelling reason for being in college? Are you a "wandering generality" or a "meaningful specific"? A wandering generality has no great sense of purpose. A meaningful specific does. Wandering generalities do not experience tremendous success while in college, while meaningful specifics do.

### Tip #2

The secret to motivating yourself: When you have a big enough "why," you'll always discover the "how."

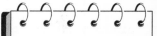

*Write this quote on an index card and tape it to your desk:*

"The thing I hate to do the most is the thing I need to do the most."

### Tip #3

Your goals are meaningless without a purpose. Define your purpose and then write it down for future reference.

## Tip #4

If your mission is to change the world, you'll never be bored.

## Tip #5

You have great things to do today, and if you don't, act as if you do!

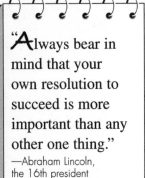

"**A**lways bear in mind that your own resolution to succeed is more important than any other one thing."
—Abraham Lincoln, the 16th president of the United States

## Tip #6

It's not good enough to do your best. In order to really succeed, you have to do *whatever it takes*.

## Tip #7

College is hard. If it were easy, everyone would have a college degree. To become a college graduate, you'll have to experience a certain amount of pain. You have a choice: Either you can experience the PAIN OF DISCIPLINE or you can experience the PAIN OF REGRET.

## Tip #8

The biggest mistake you can make in college is to drop out. HANG IN THERE! Your college degree will change your life.

## Tip #9

Your parents are counting on you. Make them proud.

## Tip #10

If you shoot for the moon and miss, at least you'll be one of the stars.

## Tip #11

The ten most powerful two-letter words:
*If it is to be, it is up to me!*

"**N**ever, never, never quit!"
—Winston Churchill, British prime minister during World War II

## Tip #12

Winners never quit, and quitters never win.

## Tip #13

Discouraged? Think about this: Michael Jordan was cut from his high school basketball team in the tenth grade.

## Tip #14

Hang on until you catch on.

## Tip #15

Anyone can handle success. The real winners learn how to handle failure.

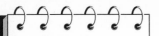

> "**O**ur greatest weakness lies in giving up. The most certain way to succeed is always to try just one more time."
>
> —Thomas Edison, inventor and entrepreneur

## Tip #16

Stop making excuses. Start working harder.

## Tip #17

College is a marathon, not a sprint. You will experience some pain along the way. For example, it's painful to study when you'd rather be out with friends. Just remember: on the day of victory, no one is tired. Which do you think would hurt more—to continue or to stop?

# What to Do in Class

## Tip #18

Don't just be *in* class—be *into* class.

## Tip #19

Are you just going to go to school or are you going to be a student? Anyone can walk into a classroom and sit at a desk. Students show up, pay attention, and act totally energized.

## Tip #20

There are three types of students:
- Those who are in the parade.
- Those who are watching the parade.
- Those who are wondering, "What parade?"

Be in the parade!

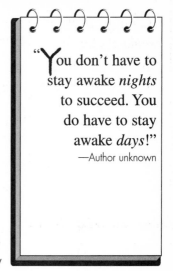

"You don't have to stay awake *nights* to succeed. You do have to stay awake *days*!"
—Author unknown

## Tip #21

The biggest mistake most students make when they go to class: they are there physically, not mentally.

## Tip #22

Act as if you are the world's greatest student:
- Sit in the middle of the front row.
- Sit up straight.
- Ask questions.
- Answer questions.
- Look interested.
- Laugh at the professor's jokes!

## Tip #23

Stay after class to discuss points of interest with your professors. This shows you're interested.

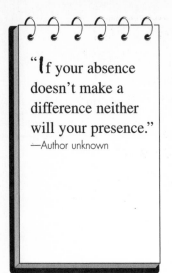

"If your absence doesn't make a difference neither will your presence."
—Author unknown

### Tip #24

Have a point of view, but don't *be* your point of view.

### Tip #25

The very first step to becoming an interesting student is to *act interested*.

### Tip #26

If you miss a class, find out what happened, get the notes from a classmate, and do the assignment right away. Being absent is *never* an excuse.

### Tip #27

Always show up early, something good is bound to happen.

### Tip #28

You'll have no competition in the classroom if you are competing for knowledge.

## Tip #29

Four questions to make this year a great school year:

1. What's the best thing that can happen to you this year?
2. What's the worst thing that can happen to you this year?
3. What can you do to make sure that the best thing does happen?
4. What can you do to make sure that the worst thing doesn't happen?

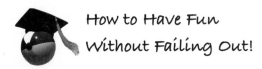

## How to Have Fun Without Failing Out!

✓ *The first rule of having fun is get involved.*
✓ **DSYNDB: Do Something You've Never Done Before.**
✓ *It's fun to go to karaoke for one night, but here's the secret: go regularly! You'll develop a new circle of friends this way. An added bonus is that when you get up in front of a group to sing, it will help prepare you for when you have to get up in front of a class to speak. Remember: no guts/no glory.*

## Chapter 2

---

**From:**      Rob Gilbert, Ph.D.

**To:**        Students

**Subject:**   Skills to Succeed

We remember what we understand; we
understand only what we pay attention
to; we pay attention to what we want.

—E. B. Bolles, writer

---

# Master Skill #1: Dealing with Professors

### Tip #30

Visit all of your professors during their office hours ASAP! It is important that your professors get to know you and that you get to know them.

### Tip #31

*Never* buy any textbook *until* the professor assigns it.

### Tip #32

Never call your professors by their first names without their permission.

### Tip #33

Call your professors *"Doctor"* even if they don't have doctorates.

### Tip #34

GUARANTEE: The easiest way to get to know a professor is to get to class early.

### Tip #35

Students like interesting professors. Professors like interesting students. Be an interesting student. If you want to be interesting—act interested.

### Tip #36

Of all the things that your professors will know about you, the most important thing they need to know is that you're a hard worker.

### Tip #37

Most professors teach because they love teaching. Take advantage of this. See if you can match their passion for teaching with your love of learning.

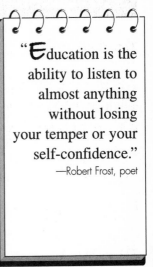

"**E**ducation is the ability to listen to almost anything without losing your temper or your self-confidence."
—Robert Frost, poet

### Tip #38

If you think a particular class is great, tell the professor.

### Tip #39

Don't believe everything you read on www.RateMyProfessor.com.

### Tip #40

Always ask your professors' permission to record their lectures. (They'll almost always be flattered!)

### Tip #41

If you are upset about a grade you got on a test, wait at least twenty-four hours before you approach your professor to argue for a better grade. If you wait, you'll be less emotional.

## Tip #42

Always talk to your professors if you see them on campus.

## Tip #43

Your best professors won't give you something to drink—they'll make you thirsty.

## Tip #44

Your professors are often more interested in your knowing "their" answers than the "right" answers.

> "One great professor can change your thinking. Many great professors can change your life."
> —The Teaching Company advertisement

## Tip #45

Be wary of professors who read exclusively from their notes; they'll expect you to remember things they don't.

## Tip #46

Make sure your professors get to know you by name.

## Tip #47

When you request a letter of recommendation from one of your professors, be sure to ask, "Will you write me a *great* letter of recommendation?" If your professor says, "Yes," you'll get a great letter of recommendation. If he or she says "No," be thankful—you wouldn't want that letter in your file anyway.

## Master Skill #2: Listening

### Tip #48

Take a lesson from the famous Broadway composer Stephen Sondheim. He was once asked how he knew so much. Sondheim replied, "I listen."

### Tip #49

Learn to *listen* by using the **LADDER** system:
- **L**ook at the person speaking.
- **A**sk questions.
- **D**on't interrupt.
- **D**on't change the subject.
- **E**mpathize.
- **R**espond verbally and nonverbally.

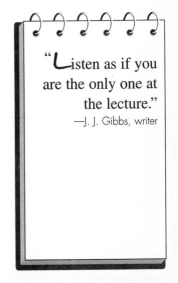

"**L**isten as if you are the only one at the lecture."
—J. J. Gibbs, writer

### Tip #50

Learn how to listen. Listen so you can learn.

## Master Skill #3: Reading

### Tip #51

Where is your mind right now? It should be right here. PAY ATTENTION! While you're reading, keep your mind on what you are doing while you are doing it.

## Típ #52

Before you read another page in any textbook learn the **Survey Q3R** Technique:

- **S**urvey the entire reading assignment—give yourself a "preview of coming attractions."
- **Q**uestion yourself about the text. After every couple of pages, ask yourself: "What is the author trying to tell me?"
- **R**ead actively by *underlining* key words, phrases, and main points.
- **R**ecite key ideas. Stop periodically and recite from memory the main points the author is making.
- **R**eview the reading assignment several times before the exam.

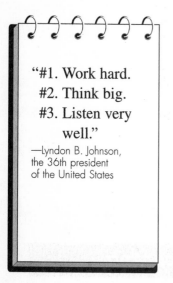

"#1. Work hard.
#2. Think big.
#3. Listen very well."

—Lyndon B. Johnson, the 36th president of the United States

## Típ #53

If you don't understand one word, you won't understand the sentence it's in.
If you don't understand the sentence, you won't understand the paragraph.
If you don't understand the paragraph, you won't understand the page.
If you don't understand the page, you won't understand the chapter.
If you don't understand the chapter, you won't understand the book.
If you don't understand the book, you'll flunk the test.
If you flunk the test, you'll get an F in the course.
*Realize that you got an F all because you didn't look up that one little word.*

## Master Skill #4: Asking Questions

### Tip #54

**NSAQ** = **N**ever **S**top **A**sking **Q**uestions.

### Tip #55

The only stupid question is the one not asked.

### Tip #56

Here's a good question to ask people you respect: "What do you know now that you wish you had known when you were in college?"

"The secret to getting a good college education: ask good questions."
—Dr. John Barrell, professor emeritus, Montclair State University

### Tip #57

Question your answers.

## Master Skill #5: Writing

### Tip #58

Avoid writing in the passive voice. It should not be used by you. ("You should not use it" sounds better, right?)

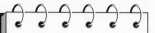

> "**P**lanning to write is not writing. Outlines . . . researching . . . talking to people about what you're doing, none of that is writing. Writing is writing."
>
> —E. L. Doctorow, writer

## Tip #59

Write in simple sentences. Sentences should never be more than sixteen to twenty words.

## Tip #60

If you don't *rite good*, find the writing clinic on campus that will teach you to *write well*.

 **Required Reading:** *The Elements of Style*, Fourth Edition, by William Strunk, Jr., and E. B. White (Longman, 1999).

## Tip #61

Don't use *its* when you mean *it's*. *It's* is the contraction of *it is*. *Its* is the possessive form of the pronoun *it*.

## Tip #62

Know the difference between *discrete* and *discreet*. Don't know the difference? Look these words up now!

## Tip #63

In writing and speaking, don't use the word "so" so much.

## Tip #64

Don't be redundant—for example, don't write or say, "*A couple of twins, a round circle, killed dead, autobiography of my life, repeat again.*"

## Tip #65

Avoid gender-specific language when you write. For example, "A student must do *his* assignment" can easily be changed to "Students must do *their* assignments."

## Tip #66

Learn how to spell words like *prerogative, accommodations,* and *occurrence.* Which one of these three words is spelled wrong? Don't know? Look them up!

## Tip #67

Don't use the word "irregardless."

## Tip #68

When you think you're spelling and grammar is perfect in your paper, have an English major proofread it. Pay a dollar for each mistake he or she finds. (Did you find the mistakes in the first sentence?)

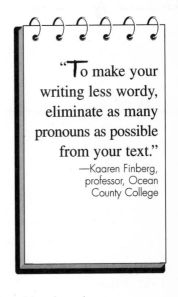

"To make your writing less wordy, eliminate as many pronouns as possible from your text."
—Kaaren Finberg, professor, Ocean County College

## Tip #69

In writing and speaking, avoid clichés like the plague.

## Tip #70

If you're waiting to get inspired to write that big paper, you'll wait forever. Schedule the time and just do it.

## Tip #71

Keep a list of the words that your computer's spellchecker regularly corrects for you and learn how to spell them.

## Tip #72

Learn how to spell by looking up words you don't know. Don't depend entirely on spellchecker.

## Tip #73

A lot of people make the mistake of using *alot*.

## Tip #74

To proofread your paper for typos and misspellings, read your paper forward and then read it backward (that's right drawkcab).

## Tip #75

For writing, spelling, and grammar questions, visit www.tcc.edu/students/resources and click on **Grammar Hotline** under the "Academics" banner. Grammar Hotline, a free service offered by Tidewater Community College in Virginia Beach, Virginia, features consultants who answer short questions during posted hours. You can also peruse the Grammar Hotline Directory, which is a list of phone numbers, e-mail addresses, and web sites you can visit for additional writing help.

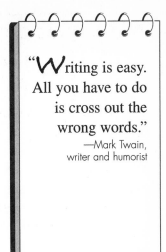

"**W**riting is easy. All you have to do is cross out the wrong words."
—Mark Twain, writer and humorist

## Master Skill #6: Time Management

## Tip #76

Practice time management. It will save you a lot of frustration in college and in life.

## Tip #77

In order to have more time for yourself, learn how to say "no" to others.

### Tip #78

Buy a time-management organizer. Use it!

### Tip #79

Get the book *First Things First: To Live, to Love, to Learn, to Leave a Legacy* by Stephen R. Covey, A. Roger Merrill, and Rebecca R. Merrill (Free Press, 1996), and learn the difference between what is *important* and what is *urgent*.

### Tip #80

For the best time-management tools, visit www.FranklinCovey.com.

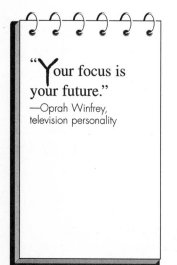

"**Y**our focus is your future."
—Oprah Winfrey,
television personality

### Tip #81

The most important thing is to make the most important thing, the most important thing.

**Required Reading:** *How to Get Control of Your Time and Your Life* by Alan Lakein (Signet, 1989).

### Tip #82

The key time-management question: *"What's the best use of my time right now?"*

## Tip #83

Make your daily study time a *planned* occurrence, not a *chance* happening.

## Tip #84

Keep your priorities straight.

## Tip #85

Plan your work, and then work your plan.

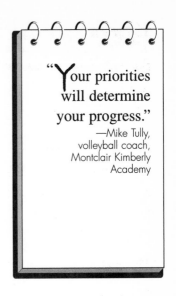

"Your priorities will determine your progress."
—Mike Tully, volleyball coach, Montclair Kimberly Academy

## Tip #86

You'll never *find* the time, but you can always *make* the time.

## Tip #87

Don't oversleep: you snooze, you lose!

## Tip #88

Don't divide your attention. Do what you're doing while you're doing it.

## Tip #89

*Energy* management is even more important than *time* management. Conserve your energy by getting adequate sleep, eating healthy foods, and using stress-reduction techniques.

## Tip #90

Study at least two hours every single day, even on weekends and holidays, *no matter what*. Do this from the first day of class until your *final* final.

## Tip #91

When you don't want to study for two hours, apply the fifteen-minute rule: study for fifteen minutes and then see how you feel.

## Tip #92

Find study partners, especially in courses you think will be particularly difficult. You will end up learning more and meeting new people.

> "**S**ometimes you'll have to force yourself to behave differently than you feel."
> —Ed Agresta, educator and motivational speaker

## Tip #93

Make a ritual of studying. Study at the same time and at the same place every day.

## Tip #94

The best place to study is the place where you won't be disturbed.

## Tip #95

Work out at the gym, eat in the cafeteria, and STUDY AT THE LIBRARY.

## Tip #96

The worst place to study is where you sleep.

"**I** discipline myself to do the things I *need* to do when I *need* to do them because I know that doing them will enable me someday to do the things I *want* to do when I *want* to do them."

—Zig Ziglar, motivational speaker

## Tip #97

For your most difficult classes, read related blogs and Google articles—anything to gain a greater understanding of the subject.

## Tip #98

At some point during the first three weeks of school, spend twelve hours in a room reading and reviewing your textbooks and notebooks. Take bathroom and food breaks only—no phone calls, radio, computer, television, or friends—just you and your books. Most students think that this is impossible. Once you do this exercise, you'll have new respect for your academic endurance, and studying for two hours a day will be cake.

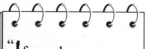 **Required Reading:** *How to Study* by Ronald W. Fry (Career Press Inc., 1996).

### Tip #99

Review . . . review . . . review.

### Tip #100

Failing to prepare is preparing to fail.

### Tip #101

Take a five- to ten-minute break for every forty to forty-five minutes you study.

> "If you have an important point to make, don't try to be subtle or clever. Use a pile driver."
> —Winston Churchill, British prime minister during World War II

### Tip #102

Keep your promises. This shows friends, family, and acquaintances that you are reliable.

### Tip #103

Flash cards are great study aids.

### Tip #104

During the first two weeks of the semester, study as hard as you would during the last two weeks of the semester.

## Tip #105

Study the most difficult material first.

## Tip #106

If you really want to see if you know something, teach it to someone else.

## Tip #107

Stop thinking like a *student* and start thinking like a *teacher*. When preparing for an exam, pretend you're the professor and make up the exam.

> "A man's command of language is most important. Next to kissing, it's the most exciting form of communication mankind has evolved."
> —Oren Arnold, writer

## Master Skill #8: Public Speaking

## Tip #108

If you're scared to death when you have to give a talk or an oral presentation—don't worry. This is proof that you're human. The secret: feel the fear and do it anyway!

## WOULD YOU *REALLY* RATHER DIE?

*According to surveys, the number-one fear in America is speaking in front of an audience. In fact, there's an old Jerry Seinfeld routine about this. Here's what Jerry said:*

*"According to most studies, people's number-one fear is public speaking. Number two is death. Death is number two. Does that sound right? This means that the average person attending a funeral would rather be in the casket than deliver the eulogy!"*

"**W**ise men talk because they have something to say; fools talk because they have to say something."
—Saul Bellow, writer

## Tip #109

Take a public speaking class during your *first* year. WARNING: If you don't take this advice—you'll regret it.

## Tip #110

Learn how to pause when you speak. Notice how you can use pausing to get two totally different meanings from this sentence:

"Woman without her man is miserable."
"Woman, without her, man is miserable."

## Tip #111

Radio personality Paul Harvey is a master at using "the pause." Listen to him nationwide on the ABC radio network or at www.PaulHarvey.com.

## Tip #112

To communicate better, be specific.

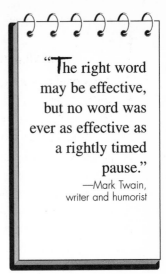

"The right word may be effective, but no word was ever as effective as a rightly timed pause."

—Mark Twain, writer and humorist

 **How to Have Fun Without Failing Out!**

✓ Join a study group with students who take class and school seriously; you'll be less inclined to slack off in their presence.

✓ Don't forget to reward yourself after studying. Positive reinforcement never fails, even if you're the one giving it to you.

# Chapter 3

**From:**     Rob Gilbert, Ph.D.

**To:**       Students

**Subject:**  Classes & Courses

Knowledge is power and teachers give it away for free!

—Author unknown

## Tip #113

Take courses with the best professors, not the easiest ones.

## Tip #114

Make at least one friend in each of your classes.

## Tip #115

Even if you think a class is boring, try to act interested.

## Tip #116

Take a yoga class. You'll increase your flexibility and learn relaxation techniques that will last a lifetime.

## Tip #117

Get all of your assignments in on time or early.

## Tip #118

Take a course at another college. Variety is the spice of life!

## Tip #119

Go to summer school. You'll graduate sooner or be able to take a lighter course load during the year.

## Tip #120

Every semester take one course simply because it interests you and not because it fulfills a requirement.

## Tip #121

Learn about the world's major religions. You will broaden your understanding of others and what is going on in the world.

## Tip #122

Don't be intimidated by graduate students—they're probably more nervous than you are!

## Tip #123

You are required to do well in your required courses. However, you are not required to like them.

## Tip #124

Keep asking the same question until *at least* two people give you the same answer.

## Tip #125

Instead of choosing a course based on when it meets, choose your courses based on the professors with the best reputations. Some students wouldn't take a course on religion at 8:00 AM even if were taught by Professor J. Christ!

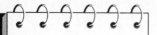

> "*O*rganic chemistry is like a sewer. What you put into it is what you'll get out of it, and it usually smells bad."
> —Seen on a button

### Tip #126

Talk in class, but don't socialize in class.

### Tip #127

Confusion is good: it means you're on the brink of learning something new.

### Tip #128

Review your notes *before* your next class, not just before an exam.

---

### AN EDUCATION ON THE HIGH SEAS

*Imagine traveling around the world on a cruise ship and getting college credit! The Semester at Sea Program is sponsored by the University of Virginia. For information, visit www.semesteratsea.com.*

---

### Tip #129

Spend your junior year abroad or go on an exchange program.

### Tip #130

It's impossible to learn what you think you already know. Be open-minded about knowledge.

### Tip #131

The most important thing you can learn in college is to learn how to learn.

### Tip #132

Don't be taught—learn.

> "I find that a great part of the information I have was acquired by looking up something and finding something else on the way."
> —Franklin P. Adams, journalist and radio personality

### Tip #133

The most exciting thing in education is discovering how much you don't know you don't know. The more you know, the more you realize you don't know.

### Tip #134

How do you eat an elephant? One bite at a time. Break large amounts of information into small, bite-sized chunks. What's easier for you to remember, the number 9,737,434,690 or the phone number (973) 743-4690?

## Tip #135

No matter how big the task:

1. Break it down.
2. Begin it now.

## Tip #136

The five ABSOLUTE ESSENTIALS you *must* learn in college:

1. Write well.
2. Speak well in front of a group.
3. Get along with others and become a great team player.
4. Access/research information quickly via computer and by contacting experts over the phone.
5. BYOB (Be Your Own Boss).

## Tip #137

Learn from the mistakes of others—you don't have to make these same mistakes yourself.

## Tip #138

You're in college to DEVELOP your mind, not just USE it.

## Tip #139

Be open-minded.

## Tip #140

It's not what you don't know that gets you in trouble. It's what you do "know" that isn't true.

# Develop Your Mental Power by Thinking Outside the Box

## Tip #141

Build your mental muscles. Here are a couple of brain teasers for you to solve:

### Exercise #1
By moving one digit make this equation correct:
$101 - 102 = 1$. See answer below.

### Exercise #2
Turn the Roman numeral IX into 6 by using just one line. See answer below.

### Exercise #3
What letter comes next in the following sequence: OTTFFSSEN? See answer below.

# What You Need to Know About Computers

## Tip #142

The first rule of computers:

*Never drink or eat near your computer.*

## Tip #143

The second rule of computers:

*Save your work every fifteen minutes.*

---

Exercise #3. T (each letter stands for the first letter of the numbers one to ten)

**Answers:** Exercise #1. $101 - 10^2 = 1$   Exercise #2. SIX

## Tip #144

The third rule of computers:
*Make backup copies of your files on a regular basis.*

## Tip #145

Reread the second rule of computers!

## Tip #146

Use a spellchecker to check your documents, but don't become dependent upon it. Don't be computer literate without also being literate!

## Tip #147

Don't miss any opportunity to learn everything you can about computers.

## Tip #148

Master Microsoft Word, Excel, and PowerPoint. You will need one or more of these skills when you begin your career.

## Tip #149

Learn how to create, maintain, and update your own website.

## Dramatically Improve Your Memory

### Tip #150

Reading is not retaining. Just because you've read something doesn't mean you've *retained* it. If you read something and don't remember it, it doesn't matter that you've read it.

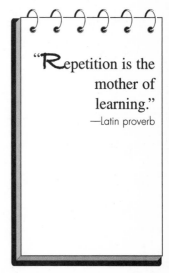

**Required Reading:** *The Memory Book: The Classic Guide to Improving Your Memory at Work, at School, and at Play* by Harry Lorayne and Jerry Lucas (Ballantine Books, 1996).

"**R**epetition is the mother of learning."
—Latin proverb

### Tip #151

The first rule of retention:

Pay attention!

**JOKE:** *He was so poor, he couldn't even pay attention!*

---

### THREE CAUSES OF "FORGETTERY"

1. *You don't get it. (If you don't get it, you can't keep it.)*
2. *You don't care. (You only remember what you want to remember.)*
3. *You don't believe. (You don't believe you already have an extraordinary memory.)*

*—Matt DiMaio, memory expert*

---

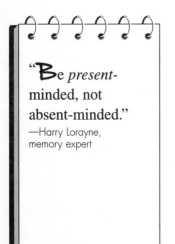

"**B**e *present-*minded, not absent-minded."
—Harry Lorayne, memory expert

### Típ #152

You have a great memory, but you might not have a *well-trained* memory.

### Típ #153

The quickest and easiest way to remember information is to use your imagination. And you have a world-class imagination! Don't believe me—let me prove it to you. Right now, try to imagine something you can't imagine. It's impossible! You can imagine anything—you DO have a world-class imagination!

# ACME

To use your imagination to improve your memory, just remember the acronym **ACME**.

**ACME** = **A**ction, **C**olor, **M**e, **E**xaggerate

To remember something better, you can make a story out of its various elements. Make sure the story has **A**ction, make it **C**olorful, put **M**e in it (that's you; see yourself in the story), and **E**xaggerate it (make it much bigger or much smaller than it really is).

Take a look at the following number. How long do you think it would take you to memorize it?

### 29350070417761307110660551225

By using your world-class imagination and **ACME**, you can memorize it in less than three minutes. Here goes. . . .

There are **29** numbers in this series, and you're going to use your imagination to memorize this string of numbers in less than **3** minutes. Guaranteed. Here's the story that goes with it:

Currently, there are **50** states in the United States. But on **07/04/1776** (July 4, 1776—the birth date of the United States), there were only **13** colonies. So, you're off to Philadelphia for a big, potluck dinner, and you're expected to bring dessert. You had a great idea—get some Slurpees. But you couldn't, because way back then, there were no (**0**) 7-Eleven (**711**) stores.

You couldn't drive to the party because there was no (**0**) Route **66**. People were driving like maniacs because there was no (**0**) **55** mile-per-hour speed limit. And with all these problems, you didn't get to the party until **12/25** (December 25)—Christmas day.

See how easy that was! The human mind loves and remembers stories. The more creative and imaginative the stories, the more memorable they will be.

### Tip #154

The most important thing your teachers never taught you about memorization:

*You don't remember words and numbers, but you do remember pictures and visual images. To memorize material, paint word-pictures in your mind.*

### Tip #155

Mnemonics are memory aids that will help turn your brain from Teflon into Velcro. Don't let information slide off your brain when you can make it stick to your brain by using these techniques.

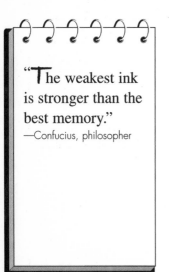

"The weakest ink is stronger than the best memory."
—Confucius, philosopher

### Tip #156

Use acronyms as memory aids:

**HOMES** = **H**uron, **O**ntario, **M**ichigan, **E**rie, **S**uperior (the Great Lakes)

**ROY G. BIV** = **R**ed, **O**range, **Y**ellow, **G**reen, **B**lue, **I**ndigo, **V**iolet (the colors of the spectrum)

"*O*ur average brain capacity is 2.8 x $10^{20}$, or approximately 10 million volumes [books] of 1,000 pages each. This outrageous capacity mandates humility. I've heard people lament that they couldn't learn any more, that their 'brain is full.' Yeah, right! There is no way that their brain is full. They have simply reached a point of fatigue and need a break for things to settle. Then, just as the body yearns for more once the last meal has been digested, we are always ready to learn more. I've never met a person who has reached the limits of his or her capacity to learn. I have, however, met plenty of folks who have quit learning."

—From *The Owner's Manual for the Brain*
by Pierce J. Howard, Ph.D.

## Tip #157

Compete for knowledge, not for grades.

> "To those of you who received honors, awards, and distinctions, I say well done. And to the C students, I say you, too, may one day be president of the United States."
> —George W. Bush, the 43rd president of the United States

## Tip #158

Make learning more important than grades.

## Tip #159

Many students only visit their professors when they want to complain about their grades. DON'T DO THIS! Do you want your professor to see you as a whiner or a winner?

## Tip #160

If you concentrate on learning, the grades will take care of themselves.

---

### AN INTERESTING FACT

*First-year students study the most and get the lowest grades. Seniors study the least and get the highest grades. As you go through college, you learn how to learn.*

## Tip #161

Aim for excellence, not perfection. (There are some students who wouldn't be happy with a 97 percent on an exam if someone else in the class got a 98 percent. This is a *big* mistake. Don't be a perfectionist.)

> "The closest I ever got to a 4.0 in college was my blood-alcohol content."
> —Seen on a bumper sticker

## Tip #162

If you really want to be a doctor, you don't have to *love* organic chemistry and physics—you just have to get an A or B in these courses.

# Cheating and Stealing: How to End Your College Career Almost Instantly

## Tip #163

Never cheat. No matter what—NEVER CHEAT!

## Tip #164

At some colleges and universities, if you get a D or an F, you can retake the course to improve your grade. So why cheat and risk expulsion?

### Tip #165

It's better to get an F than to cheat. An F only signifies a *lack of preparation*. Cheating signifies a *lack of character*.

### Tip #166

Borrowing without permission is stealing. Never steal even the smallest item.

### Tip #167

Don't even think of taking something from the college bookstore without paying for it.

## The Moment of Truth: Taking Tests

### Tip #168

If you really must miss an exam, always inform your professor *beforehand*.

### Tip #169

When you're taking an exam and you can't remember something—don't panic! Take a deep breath and repeat this phrase three times: "It will come to me."

## Tip #170

The night before an exam, make up your own exam questions and answer them. It's even better if you do this with others; everybody should bring their own exam questions, and then you can answer them as a group.

"**G**etting testy during a test will not help you do your best."
—Sue Burghard Brooks, editor

## Tip #171

On multiple-choice and true/false exams, go with your gut: your first answer is usually the best answer.

## Tip #172

On essay exams, turn up the volume: Write more, not less. And write neatly.

## Tip #173

When taking an exam, answer the easy questions *first*.

## Tip #174

Don't spend too much time on any one question.

## Tip #175

The Golden Rule of Partial Credit:
>        *Never leave an exam question unanswered.*

## Tip #176

You've been studying all night. You're exhausted, and you have that important exam in just a few hours. Take a shower and get dressed in your best clothes. You'll feel energized!

---

### A POP QUIZ

I'll bet you weren't expecting a quiz! In the spaces below, write down three ideas you've learned from this book so far that can help make you a better student.

1. _____

2. _____

3. _____

Now here's the real quiz:

1. *CAN* you do these three things?     Yes     No

2. *WILL* you do these three things?     Yes     No

3. *WHEN* will you start doing these three things?

    Immediately          Later Today          Tomorrow

---

## Tip #177

The difference between *can* and *will* is the difference between graduating and not graduating. *Can* you carry out the suggestions in this book? Of course you can! *Will* you carry them out? This is the key question.

## Tip #178

Don't just USE the strategies you learn from this book. CONSISTENTLY USE them on a daily basis. In other words, make a HABIT of them.

## Tip #179

The one-word course in college success:

*Curiosity*

## Tip #180

The one-word course in getting great grades:

*Overprepare*

## Tip #181

The one-word course in earning your college degree:

*Commitment*

---

### STUDY BREAK #1

*You need at least one great trivia question about the movies. If you don't have any, use this one:*

*QUESTION: Name the seven dwarfs.*

*ANSWER: See below.*

---

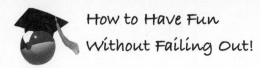

# How to Have Fun
# Without Failing Out!

✓ *Major in something that is fun and interesting. You might think this is obvious, but surprisingly, most people don't do this.*

✓ *If you really want to make some memories, spend a semester or year studying abroad. My suggestion: find a college or university in Australia.*

✓ *A college campus is teeming with all types of "temptations" that might "seduce" you. Repeat after me: "College is NOT all about fun." Don't try to cram four years of fun into your first semester! Remember: everything in moderation.*

✓ *Ask juniors and seniors about the most fun class they ever took—and take it!*

# Chapter 4

---

**From:**     Rob Gilbert, Ph.D.

**To:**       Students

**Subject:**  Homework & Assignments

Spectacular achievements are always pre-
ceded by unspectacular preparation.

—Roger Staubach, pro-football superstar

---

### Tip #182

It's the *start* that *stops* most people.

### Tip #183

How do you get started? By getting started. You don't have to feel like it to do it. But once you start doing it— you'll feel like it.

### Tip #184

The four-letter solution to procrastination:

**DO**n't wa**IT**!

### Tip #185

The most difficult part of *any* assignment is how difficult you make it for yourself.

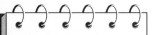

**"N**othing is particularly hard if you divide it into small jobs."
—Henry Ford, founder of the Ford Motor Company

### Tip #186

If you don't have time to do the assignment right, when are you going to find the time to take the course over?

### Tip #187

Do assigned readings *before* class.

## Tip #188

Spend the extra money and print your assignments on high-quality paper.

## Creating Great Habits

## Tip #189

Human beings are habit-taking-on machines. Great students have great habits. Dr. William James, the father of American psychology, developed three steps for how to start a great habit:

1. Start immediately.
2. Do it flamboyantly.
3. No exceptions.

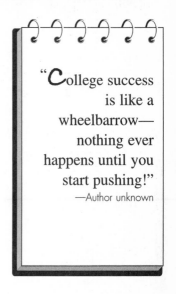

"*C*ollege success is like a wheelbarrow—nothing ever happens until you start pushing!"
—Author unknown

## Tip #190

You become what you repeatedly do. So repeat positive things like studying, exercising, and eating healthy.

## Tip #191

If it's easy to do, it's also easy *not* to do.

## Tip #192

Want to graduate *summa cum laude*? Turn your TV-watching habit into a studying habit. The average college student watches twenty-three hours of TV per week. Imagine if you put that time toward studying!

### Tip #193

Most people watch television as if they were getting paid for it! Instead, why don't you study and do your assignments as if you were getting paid for it.

### Tip #194

**DWYSYWD** = **D**o **W**hat **Y**ou **S**ay **Y**ou **W**ill **D**o.

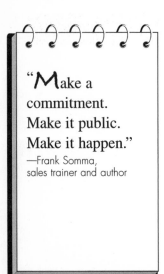

"**M**ake a commitment. Make it public. Make it happen."
—Frank Somma, sales trainer and author

### Tip #195

Poor study habits turn into poor grades.

### Tip #196

Good study habits turn into good grades.

### Tip #197

Great study habits turn into great grades.

### Tip #198

Better fifteen minutes early than one minute late. Make "early" a habit.

## Tip #199

You don't decide when the class begins. The professor decides when the class begins. Be on time—all the time!

"Your memory is made of paper, keep great notes."
—John M. Capozzi, entrepreneur and author

## Results, Not Excuses

### Tip #200

If you are late to class and you have an excuse—you're still late.

### Tip #201

If you cut class and you have an excuse—you're still absent.

### Tip #202

If you turn in an assignment after it's due and you have an excuse—it's still late.

## Little Things That'll Make a Big Difference

### Tip #203

When you take notes, circle and put stars around *everything* the professor writes on the board.

"There are many hard things in life. There is only one sad thing—giving up."
—Susan Butcher, champion dogsled racer

### Tip #204

Learn mindmapping. Have no idea what this is? A good place to start is with the book *Mindmapping: Your Personal Guide to Exploring Creativity and Problem-Solving* by Joyce Wycoff (Berkley Trade,1991).

### Tip #205

Buy a small dictionary. Keep it with you at all times. Look up every word you don't know.

## Tip #206

Do a little every day. "Inch by inch, it's a cinch, but yard by yard, it might be hard."

## Tip #207

Photocopy your student ID, your credit cards, and anything else in your wallet that's important. Keep these copies in a safe place.

## Tip #208

Doing *a little a lot* is much more effective than doing *a lot a little*.

## Tip #209

Make friends with your department's secretary. This person will be a very valuable ally in the near future.

## THE ASSIGNMENT

*Sid Bernstein worked in the entertainment business in New York City and was also a graduate student at the New School. When he took a course with the famous journalist Max Lerner, he was required to read a foreign newspaper every week. For his first assignment, Bernstein read a London paper and saw a small article about a British rock group.*

*The next week there was a bigger article about the same group. The third week there was an even bigger article. These articles motivated him to make several phone calls to London. After making the proper business contacts, Sid Bernstein got the rights to produce the first United States tour of this British rock group—The Beatles.*

*And it all started with a college assignment.*

## How to Have Fun Without Failing Out!

✓ *If you have fun taking notes, they'll be more "brain-friendly." Use different color pens and highlighters, draw pictures, make diagrams, use arrows—anything that brings excitement to the page.*

✓ *Volunteer to be a "subject" for a professor's research project. If you find this fun or fascinating, ask the professor how you can become more involved in the project. You might get extra credit— or you might even get paid!*

# Chapter 5

**From:** Rob Gilbert, Ph.D.

**To:** Students

**Subject:** Staying Safe, Sane, & Healthy

All the joy the world contains
Has come through wishing happiness
  for others.
All the misery the world contains
Has come through wanting pleasure
  for oneself.

—Shantideva,
8th-century Buddhist scholar

### Tip #210

If you want to lose weight, follow this five-word formula: Eat less and exercise more.

### Tip #211

Start eating right—right now!

"**N**othing tastes as good as thin feels."
—Weight Watchers slogan

### Tip #212

Eat less red meat.

### Tip #213

Eat less fat.

### Tip #214

Don't take the campus bus—walk.

### Tip #215

If you drive, you must follow the first rule of driving:
*Buckle Up!*

### Tip #216

Never eat pizza after 10:00 PM.

### Tip #217

Drink eight 8-ounce glasses of water every day.

### Tip #218

Don't smoke. If you do smoke—**STOP**!

### Tip #219

The first rule of quitting smoking:
*Don't Start.*

### Tip #220

Want to get healthier and lose weight almost instantly? Start basing your diet on the fourteen superfoods described in *SuperFoods Rx: Fourteen Foods That Will Change Your Life* by Steven G. Pratt, M.D., and Kathy Matthews (Harper Paperbacks, 2005). The superfoods are:

"Those of you who do not find time for exercise sooner or later will have to find time for illness."
—The Earl of Derby

- beans
- blueberries
- broccoli
- oats
- oranges
- pumpkin
- soy
- spinach
- tea (green or black)
- tomatoes
- turkey breast, skinless
- walnuts
- wild salmon
- yogurt

### Tip #221

Most college students are sleep-deprived. If you want to solve this problem, read *Power Sleep: The Revolutionary Program That Prepares Your Mind for Peak Performance* by James B. Maas, Megan L. Wherry, David J. Axelrod, and Barbara R. Hogan (Collins, 1999). This book will teach you how to get "more A's with zzz's."

## Relax and Win

### Tip #222

If you're too busy to relax—you're too busy.

"The picture of health needs a good frame of mind."

—Seen on a sign outside a church

### Tip #223

It's not what's happening *around* you. It's not what's happening *to* you. What really matters is what's happening *inside* you.

### Tip #224

Your breath is the key to relaxation. You can never be relaxed when you're breathing quickly, and you can never be tense when you're breathing slowly.

## Tip #225

Be intense without being tense. You have to care, but not too much.

## Tip #226

Two rules that will help you keep your sanity (and sense of humor):

Rule #1: Don't sweat the small stuff.

Rule #2: Realize it's all small stuff.

"**A** light heart lives long."
—William Shakespeare, English poet and playwright

**Required Reading:** *The Relaxation Response* by Herbert Benson, M.D. (Harper Paperbacks, 2000) and *The Precious Present* by Spencer Johnson (Doubleday, 1984).

## Tip #227

Put the Serenity Prayer in a place where you'll see it: "God grant me the serenity to accept the things I cannot change, courage to change the things I can, and wisdom to know the difference."

## Tip #228

What's it going to be, *skills* or *pills*? If you don't learn the *skills* of relaxation, eventually you're going to need the *pills* for relaxation.

**Required Listening:** Johann Pachelbel's *Canon in D.*

## Sex

### Tip #229

Take a course or workshop in sex education.

### Tip #230

If you live on a co-ed floor, don't have a sexual relationship with any of your floor mates.

### Tip #231

Learn about safe sex.

### Tip #232

Practice safe sex.

### Tip #233

Never "sexile" your roommate(s), and never allow your roommate(s) to "sexile" you. Confused? *Sexiling* is when you're exiled from your room because a roommate is having sex.

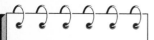

"**S**ex is the one thing that takes up the least amount of time and causes the most amount of trouble."
—John Barrymore, actor

### Tip #234

Learn about birth control.

### Tip #235

Practice birth control.

### Tip #236

Learn about AIDS and other sexually transmitted diseases.

### Tip #237

If you don't want to have sex—DON'T! You have the right to say, "No."

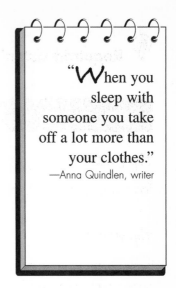

"**W**hen you sleep with someone you take off a lot more than your clothes."
—Anna Quindlen, writer

### Tip #238

Never, ever sleep with someone on the first date.

### Tip #239

Learn how to kiss.

## Your New Home: Living in Residence Halls

### Tip #240

Don't hang around your residence hall between 3:00 PM and 6:00 PM. Try out for an athletic team, work out, get a part-time job, or go to the library. Don't just "veg out."

## Tip #241

Make friends with the maintenance workers. You'll never know when you might need them.

## Tip #242

Many thefts happen during the first two weeks of the semester. Keep your door locked!

## Tip #243

Don't stay in your room on Friday nights.

## Tip #244

Always keep your room locked when you're not there.

## Tip #245

Don't keep a television in your room. Study instead.

## Tip #246

One of the best experiences you can have is to become a resident assistant.

# Getting Along with Roommates

### Típ #247

Treat your roommates as if they were your best friends, even if they aren't.

### Típ #248

If your roommate smells, don't suffer. Gently tell him or her.

### Típ #249

NEVER flirt with your boyfriend's/girlfriend's roommate.

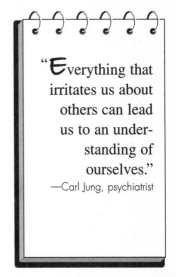

"**E**verything that irritates us about others can lead us to an understanding of ourselves."

—Carl Jung, psychiatrist

### Típ #250

NEVER flirt with your roommate's boyfriend/girlfriend.

### Típ #251

Trust me: For your first semester in college, DO NOT have a friend from home as your roommate.

## Never, Never, Never

### Típ #252

Never hitchhike.

### Tip #253

The best tip you'll ever receive about gambling:

*Don't.*

### Tip #254

Never read a newspaper in class.

### Tip #255

No all-nighters!

### Tip #256

Never wear T-shirts with offensive messages.

### Tip #257

Never miss a class. Okay, *almost* never miss a class.

### Tip #258

Procrastinate procrastinating: Put off putting things off.

### Tip #259

Never forget Mother's Day.

### Tip #260

Your higher education should not include getting "high." Never take recreational drugs. Before you object to this, Google "Len Bias" and read his tragic story.

## Tip #261

Never walk alone at night in poorly lit sections of the campus. Find out if campus security provides an escort service, and if they do, take advantage of it.

## Tip #262

Never plagiarize. Before you even consider it, check out the website www.turnitin.com.

## Tip #263

Never get involved with a cult. Be aware of cult groups on campus. For additional information, visit:
www.CultsOnCampus.com.

## Tip #264

Never tell jokes that are racist, sexist, or antigay.

## Tip #265

Never laugh at or encourage jokes that are racist, sexist, or antigay.

## Tip #266

Never correct professors in a way that might embarrass them.

### Tip #267

Never gossip.

### Tip #268

Never miss an opportunity to be kind.

## $$$ Finances $$$

### Tip #269

If you think education is expensive—try ignorance.

"I had plastic surgery last week. I cut up my credit card."
—Henny Youngman, comedian

### Tip #270

Don't borrow money—lend.

### Tip #271

Don't exceed the minutes allowed on your cell-phone plan or your phone bill might become higher than your tuition!

### Tip #272

Don't expect scholarships and awards to beg you to apply for them.

### Tip #273

You need only *one* credit card.
Don't use it frivolously.

### Tip #274

Don't spend more money than
you have. You don't want to
spend your adult life paying off
credit card debt from your
college days.

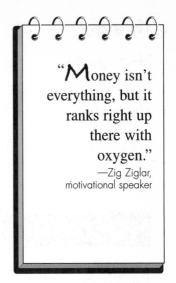

> "**M**oney isn't
> everything, but it
> ranks right up
> there with
> oxygen."
> —Zig Ziglar,
> motivational speaker

### Tip #275

You may be an "A" student with fabulous references, but if
you have a bad credit rating, there's a good chance you
won't get the job you want after college. (Your credit score
shows the world how responsible you are.)

### Tip #276

The best place to buy and sell textbooks online is
www.half.com.

## Don't Be Afraid to Ask for Help

### Tip #277

Visit your advisor and ask for advice even if you don't think
you need it.

## Tip #278

Learn how to ask for help. No one ever made it through college alone.

## Tip #279

Get academic advisement every semester.

## Tip #280

Write down everything an academic advisor tells you. Also write down the name of the advisor and the date of your meeting. Keep these notes in case you receive conflicting information.

## Tip #281

Don't miss any opportunities to help others. Offer your notes to students who've missed class. Tutor classmates who need help.

## Tip #282

You won't succeed if others fail. You'll succeed if you help others succeed. As Father James Keller of The Christophers said, "A candle loses nothing by lighting another candle."

## Tip #283

Make friends with a research librarian.

## Tip #284

Realize there are staff members on campus who are there to help you solve your biggest problems.

## Tip #285

Get a tutor *before* you need one.

## Tip #286

If you are, or think you might be, anorexic or bulimic, GET HELP IMMEDIATELY! One place to start is with an on-campus counseling center.

> "Before everything else, getting ready is the secret of success."
> —Henry Ford, founder of the Ford Motor Company

## Tip #287

A book that has gotten many people through some very tough times is *How to Survive the Loss of a Love* by Peter McWilliams, Harold H. Bloomfield, and Melba Colgrove (Prelude Press, 1993).

## Tip #288

Get a mentor. A mentor is a person whose *hindsight* can become your *foresight*. Your "ideal" mentor would be a junior or senior in your major with a GPA greater than 3.0.

## Tip #289

If you have, or even think you might have, a drinking problem, go to an Alcoholics Anonymous meeting. Many colleges and universities have AA meetings right on campus.

## Tip #290

Many students are in denial about alcoholism on campus. They believe there aren't any alcoholics in college, just people who love to party.

## Tip #291

If you feel like you're getting the runaround from professors or school administrators, ask them this question: "What would you do if you were in my situation?"

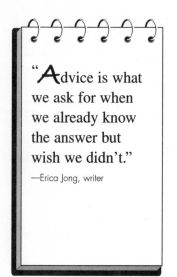

"Advice is what we ask for when we already know the answer but wish we didn't."

—Erica Jong, writer

## Tip #292

Learn how to recognize the symptoms of depression in yourself and others. Some of the symptoms include fatigue, difficulty concentrating, negative feelings, changes in appetite or weight, loss of interest in pleasurable things, recurring physical problems, persistent sadness, restlessness, irritability, sleep problems, and thoughts of suicide.

## Tip #293

Are you depressed? If so, see a counselor at your school's psychological services office. Don't wait. The sooner you get an appointment, the quicker you'll start feeling better.

## Tip #294

Suicide is a permanent solution to a temporary problem. If you feel suicidal—get help immediately.

## How to Have Fun Without Failing Out!

✓ *Buy the bestselling relaxation CD of all time: "Letting Go of Stress" by Emmett Miller, M.D., and Steven Halpern.*

✓ *Surprise friends in your residence hall by festively decorating their doors on their birthdays.*

✓ *Make a habit of going to the fitness center on campus. You'll meet new people and get in great shape.*

✓ *Spring Break is a must! You don't have to go to an exotic destination, but you do need to take a break.*

✓ *If your Spring Break plans include non-stop partying, be smart. Don't do anything that could ruin your reputation or future—or that you wouldn't want grandma and grandpa to see on TV.*

**Answer:** Elvis

# Chapter 6

**From:** Rob Gilbert, Ph.D.

**To:** Students

**Subject:** Making Time for Fun

Be quick, but don't hurry.

—John Wooden, the most successful coach
in college basketball history

## Tip #295

Here's a great way to tell if you're in love: Dr. Seuss once said, "You know you're in love when you can't fall asleep because reality is finally better than your dreams."

## Tip #296

There's a big difference between saying "**I** love you," and "I love **YOU**."

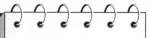

"The deepest principle in human nature is the craving to be appreciated."
—William James, professor of psychology and philosophy, Harvard

## Tip #297

Love your partner when they deserve it least, because that's when they need it most.

## Tip #298

The Golden Rule is wrong. Don't treat others the way *you* want to be treated. Treat others the way *they* want to be treated.

## Tip #299

The most interesting people may not always be the best looking.

## Tip #300

The best-looking people may not always be the most interesting.

## Tip #301

Disagree without being disagreeable.

## Tip #302

People of low intelligence talk about other people.
People of average intelligence talk about things.
People of high intelligence talk about ideas.

> "**M**anners are a sensitive awareness of the feelings of others. If you have that awareness, you have good manners, no matter what fork you use."
> —Emily Post, etiquette expert

## Tip #303

Myth: It's not what you know, it's who you know.
Truth: It's what you know, it's who you know, *and* it's who knows you.

## Tip #304

Don't go looking for that perfect person because that perfect person might also be looking for that perfect person.

### Tip #305

To understand human nature better, remember poet Maya Angelou's insight: "I've learned that people will forget what you said, people will forget what you did, but people will never forget how you made them feel."

## What's on Campus

### Tip #306

Listen to the college radio station.

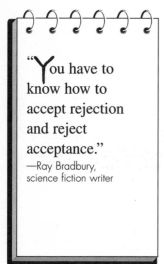

"You have to know how to accept rejection and reject acceptance."
—Ray Bradbury, science fiction writer

### Tip #307

Watch the college television station.

### Tip #308

Read the college newspaper.

### Tip #309

The most important question to ask a fraternity or sorority you're considering pledging: "How many of your brothers/sisters who graduated last spring went on to medical school, law school, MBA programs, or grad school?"

### Tip #310

Donate blood at the campus blood drive every year. You will help save lives.

### Tip #311

Get involved in an extracurricular activity you've never tried before. It's a good way to meet new people and learn more about what you like and what you don't like.

"Be careful! You might not be your best friend's best friend."
—Author unknown

### Tip #312

Join a volunteer organization. You will help others and it will help you feel good about yourself.

## Your Personal Life

### Tip #313

The first rule of having a friend is being a friend.

### Tip #314

Keep a journal, but keep it in a safe place.

### Tip #315

Stay in touch with your friends back home.

"It's a funny thing about life; if you refuse to accept anything but the best, you very often get it."
—W. Somerset Maugham, writer

### Tip #316

Write down your locker combination and keep it in a secret place.

### Tip #317

Shock your parents: write them a sincere letter thanking them for all they've done for you.

### Tip #318

Remember important birthdays and anniversaries.

### Tip #319

You're never too old to feel homesick.

### Tip #320

Observe your religious holidays.

### Tip #321

It's okay to be scared to death.

### Tip #322

Don't sleep late—even on Sundays.

# READER/CUSTOMER CARE SURVEY

We care about your opinions! Please take a moment to fill out our online Reader Survey at **http://survey.hcibooks.com**.
As a **"THANK YOU"** you will receive a **VALUABLE INSTANT COUPON** towards future book purchases as well as a **SPECIAL GIFT** available only online! Or, you may mail this card back to us and we will send you a copy of our exciting catalog with your valuable coupon inside.

(PLEASE PRINT IN ALL CAPS)

First Name _____ MI. _____ Last Name _____

Address _____ City _____

State _____ Zip _____ Email _____

**1. Gender**
- ☐ Female  ☐ Male

**2. Age**
- ☐ 8 or younger
- ☐ 9-12  ☐ 13-16
- ☐ 17-20  ☐ 21-30
- ☐ 31+

**3. Did you receive this book as a gift?**
- ☐ Yes  ☐ No

**4. Annual Household Income**
- ☐ under $25,000
- ☐ $25,000 - $34,999
- ☐ $35,000 - $49,999
- ☐ $50,000 - $74,999
- ☐ over $75,000

**5. What are the ages of the children living in your house?**
- ☐ 0 - 14  ☐ 15+

**6. Marital Status**
- ☐ Single
- ☐ Married
- ☐ Divorced
- ☐ Widowed

**7. How did you find out about the book?**
*(please choose one)*
- ☐ Recommendation
- ☐ Store Display
- ☐ Online
- ☐ Catalog/Mailing
- ☐ Interview/Review

**8. Where do you usually buy books?**
*(please choose one)*
- ☐ Bookstore
- ☐ Online
- ☐ Book Club/Mail Order
- ☐ Price Club (Sam's Club, Costco's, etc.)
- ☐ Retail Store (Target, Wal-Mart, etc.)

**9. What subject do you enjoy reading about the most?**
*(please choose one)*
- ☐ Parenting/Family
- ☐ Relationships
- ☐ Recovery/Addictions
- ☐ Health/Nutrition
- ☐ Christianity
- ☐ Spirituality/Inspiration
- ☐ Business Self-help
- ☐ Women's Issues
- ☐ Sports

**10. What attracts you most to a book?**
*(please choose one)*
- ☐ Title
- ☐ Cover Design
- ☐ Author
- ☐ Content

FOLD HERE

Comments

### Tip #323

Invite an international student to go home with you for Thanksgiving weekend.

### Tip #324

The problem with lying is that you have to remember your lies.

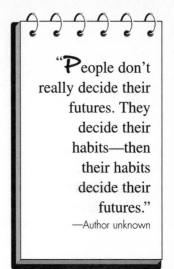

"People don't really decide their futures. They decide their habits—then their habits decide their futures."
—Author unknown

### Tip #325

Don't hang around with your high school friends during the first two weeks of college. Force yourself to meet new people and make new friends.

### Tip #326

Don't eat at the same place with the same people every day.

### Tip #327

Get in the habit of saying "you" and "your" more than "I" and "my."

### Tip #328

Become the person you want to be. Don't sell out!

### Tip #329

Hang out with people who are smarter than you.

## Tip #330

Date.

## Tip #331

Always chew with your mouth closed, especially in movie theaters.

## Tip #332

Be careful of people who *think* they have all the answers.

## Tip #333

Be tolerant. If you're straight—don't be narrow.

## Tip #334

If it sounds too good to be true, it probably is.

## Tip #335

Don't be surprised if, in the end, your biggest weakness becomes your biggest strength.

## Seven Things to Learn
## Outside of Class

### Tip #336

Learn how to meditate.

### Tip #337

Learn to play golf. (For business
majors, this is a requirement.)

### Tip #338

Learn to juggle.

### Tip #339

Learn at least one great card trick.

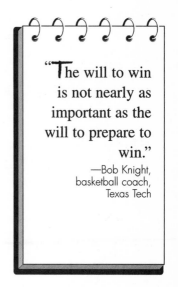

"The will to win
is not nearly as
important as the
will to prepare to
win."
—Bob Knight,
basketball coach,
Texas Tech

### Tip #340

Learn about the nonprint media resources in the library.

### Tip #341

Learn CPR.

## Tip #342

Learn all you can about stress reduction and relaxation techniques.

---

### THREE GREAT BOOKS ABOUT COLLEGE LIFE

- *I Am Charlotte Simmons* by Tom Wolfe (Picador USA, 2005)
- *Chicken Soup for the College Soul: Inspiring and Humorous Stories about College* by Jack Canfield, Mark Victor Hansen, Kimberly Kirberger, and Dan Clark (HCI, 1999)
- *College in a Can: What's in, Who's out, Where to, Why not, and Everything Else You Need to Know About Life on Campus* by Sandra Choron and Harry Choron (Houghton Mifflin, 2004)

### FIVE GREAT MOVIES ABOUT COLLEGE LIFE

- *Drumline* (2002)
- *Good Will Hunting* (1998)
- *The Graduate* (1967)
- *National Lampoon's Animal House* (1978)
- *The Paper Chase* (1973)

---

## Downtime Activities

## Tip #343

Save your soap-opera watching until May when finals are over.

### Tip #344

Watch C-SPAN.

### Tip #345

Watch Woody Allen films.

### Tip #346

Rent *Akeelah and the Bee* (2006).

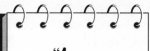

"If you're an athlete, the most important line-up you can make in college is the one at graduation."
—Oliver Gelston, basketball coach, Montclair State University

 **Required Reading:** *The College Humor Guide to College* by the writers of CollegeHumor.com (Dutton Adult, 2006).

## Sports

### Tip #347

You don't have to be a superstar to participate in intramural sports.

### Tip #348

Go to the first home football game—even if you hate football!

"Twenty years from now, people will not remember what sport you played. Twenty years from now, people will not remember if you were any good or not. But twenty years from now, as soon as you open your mouth, people will know whether or not you got an education."

—The Rev. Theodore Hesburgh, president emeritus of the University of Notre Dame, in a speech to his athletes

### Tip #349

Meet your heroes who are still living.

### Tip #350

Ask someone who intimidates you out for coffee.

### Tip #351

AIM HIGH: Win a prestigious Rhodes Scholarship.

### Tip #352

Don't skydive.

## Remember, It's Not All About Partying

### Tip #353

Start to worry when the best parties you attended are the ones you don't remember.

### Tip #354

Know when to say "when."

### Tip #355

Have fun, but make sure your college *days* don't turn into a college *daze*.

### Tip #356

If you're having too good a time, you might not survive in college for too long a time.

### Tip #357

Remember this: "If you obey all the rules, you miss all the fun!"
—Katharine Hepburn, Academy Award–winning actor

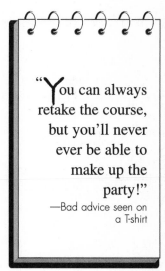

"You can always retake the course, but you'll never ever be able to make up the party!"
—Bad advice seen on a T-shirt

## "I SHOULDA"

*In my almost thirty years at Montclair State, no former student has ever come back for a visit and said, "I made a big mistake while I was here. I should have partied more!" But they have said things like, "If I had studied more, I could have gotten into medical school." Or "If I practiced harder, I could have been an All American." Or "If I worked harder on my research project, I could have had it published." So, take a lesson from them and avoid all those future shouldas and couldas.*

## How to Have Fun Without Failing Out!

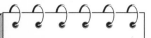

"It's not a beer belly—it's a liquid-grain storage facility."
—Seen on a T-shirt

✓ *Let your imagination go wild. Create an outrageous costume for Halloween. You won't have to find a party—you'll be the party!*

✓ *Drink for free! Buy the DVD "How to Scam Your Way to Free Beer and Other Bar Bets" by Todd Robbins.*

✓ *Want to drive a friend crazy? Secretly slide a greeting card under his or her door and sign it "from someone who thinks you're terrific." And then wait!*

✓ *For a quick adventure, take a car full of friends on a spontaneous road trip.*

## Chapter 7

**From:** Rob Gilbert, Ph.D.

**To:** Students

**Subject:** Believe in Your Abilities

The ultimate measure of a man is not where he stands in moments of comfort and convenience but where he stands at times of challenge and controversy.

—Dr. Martin Luther King, Jr.,
civil rights leader

# "I'm Not Smart Enough."

### Tip #358

You're much smarter than you think you are. You are an incredible learning machine.

### Tip #359

Success in college is a matter of *diligence*, not *intelligence*.

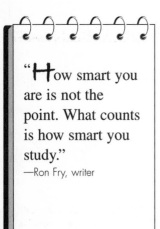

"How smart you are is not the point. What counts is how smart you study."
—Ron Fry, writer

### Tip #360

Curiosity always beats intelligence.

### Tip #361

Always remember that you have the world's most powerful computer sitting on top of your shoulders.

### Tip #362

Don't worry about how smart you are. The *smartest* students don't do as well as the *best* students.

### Tip #363

You have unlimited mental resources. The storage capacity of your brain is greater than that of all the libraries in the world put together. Reread the passage on page 43.

### Tip #364

If you think you don't belong in college—YOU'RE WRONG!

### Tip #365

If you think you don't have the *ability* to be successful in college—YOU'RE WRONG!

### Tip #366

Don't think you have all the answers.

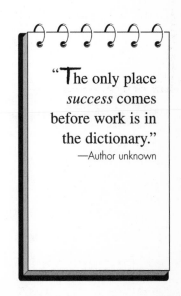

"**A** mind is a terrible thing to waste."
—The United Negro College Fund motto

### Tip #367

The disorganized genius will not do as well as the organized person with average intelligence.

### Tip #368

Your brain has an unlimited capacity for learning, memorization, and creativity.

"**T**he only place *success* comes before work is in the dictionary."
—Author unknown

### Tip #369

You've already learned difficult skills like walking, talking, and reading, so you'll have no trouble learning easier skills like using a computer, mastering a foreign language, and playing a sport.

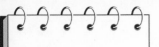

> "**N**obody who ever gave his best regretted it."
>
> —George Halas, professional football coach and owner

### Tip #370

No matter how complex the math or computer problem, it will eventually yield to the persistence of your mind.

### Tip #371

If you were smart enough to be admitted to college, you're smart enough to graduate *with honors*. Absolutely, positively guaranteed!

### Tip #372

The worst type of prejudice is the prejudice you have against yourself. Don't prejudge yourself.

### Tip #373

How to have a great idea:

*Have a lot of ideas.*

## It's All About Effort

### Tip #374

**K – A = 0**

(Knowledge without Action is Nothing)

## Tip #375

Work smart, not hard.

 **Required Reading:** *Do It! Let's Get Off Our Buts!* by Peter McWilliams (Prelude Press, 1994)

## Tip #376

Luck follows preparation.

## Tip #377

Don't say, "I can't" when you really mean "I don't want to."

## Tip #378

The two-step formula for academic excellence:

Step #1: Do more of what *does* work.
Step #2: Do less of what *doesn't* work.

> "The harder you work, the more you accomplish. The more you accomplish, the better you feel. The better you feel, the more you like it. The more you like it, the harder you work."
> —Michael Cast, professional speaker

## Tip #379

Stop making excuses.

## Tip #380

Your success is only limited by your desire. This means that it's not how good you are—it's how good you want to be.

# Don't Get Discouraged

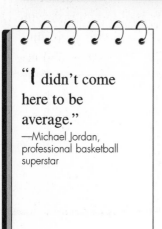

"**I** didn't come here to be average."
—Michael Jordan, professional basketball superstar

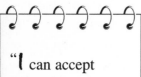

"**I** can accept failure. Everyone fails at something. But I can't accept not trying."
—Michael Jordan, professional basketball superstar

### Tip #381

When you're at the library feeling down and discouraged, go to the encyclopedia and read the biographies of Helen Keller and Abraham Lincoln.

### Tip #382

Still feel discouraged? Rent the video *Rudy* (1993).

### Tip #383

When you're feeling frustrated, depressed, or unmotivated, think about your long-term goals.

### Tip #384

Nothing positive will ever come from being negative, and nothing negative will ever come from being positive.

### Tip #385

What are you going to do when you get a low grade? What are you going to do when you get criticized or rejected? You have two choices: Are you going to get BITTER or BETTER? You'd better get BETTER!

# No Regrets

## Tip #386

Have no regrets. When you look back on your college days, make sure you can say, "I'm glad I did" not "I wish I had."

> "Confidence is the most important single factor in this game and no matter how great your natural talent there is only one way to obtain it—work."
>
> —Jack Nicklaus, professional golfer

## ADVICE FROM A GENIUS

*Albert Einstein was one of the greatest minds of all time. But believe it or not, he didn't do well in college.*
**Here's some of his advice for you . . .**

*"Imagination is more than knowledge."*

*

*"I have no particular talent; I am merely extremely inquisitive."*

*

*"I think and think for months and years. Ninety-nine times, the conclusion is false. The hundredth time I am right."*

*

*EINSTEIN'S FORMULA FOR SUCCESS:* $A = X + Y + Z$

$A$ = success

$X$ = work

$Y$ = play

$Z$ = keeping your mouth shut

> "**T**wenty years from now, you will be more disappointed by the things you didn't do than by the things you did do."
> —Mark Twain, writer and humorist

## Tip #387

The ultimate secret to creativity:
**C = MSU**
(**C**reativity = **M**aking **S**tuff **U**p)

## Tip #388

Are you one of those students who thinks you always do your best by cramming the night before the exam? It's not the best way; it's the way you're used to doing it. Have you ever tried it any other way?

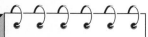

> "**C**ontinuous effort—not strength or intelligence—is the key to unlocking our potential."
> —Winston Churchill, British prime minister during World War II

## Tip #389

Practice the five Ps: Prior Preparation Prevents Poor Performance.

## Tip #390

Quitting school is not an option.

## Tip #391

The biggest question of your entire college career:
*Can you survive the first six weeks?*

## How to Have Fun Without Failing Out!

✓ If you are feeling discouraged find a friend who encourages you and go for coffee.
✓ Want to become an instant celebrity on campus? Write for the college newspaper or get a program on the college radio station.
✓ Want to see all the best plays and concerts on campus for free? Sign up to be a student usher.

"**D**on't listen to those who say you're taking too big a chance. Michelangelo would have painted the Sistine floor, and it would surely be rubbed out by today."
—Neil Simon, playwright

---

**Answer:** The day before and the day after Major League Baseball's All-Star Game.

## Chapter 8

---

**From:**     Rob Gilbert, Ph.D.

**To:**       Students

**Subject:**  Graduation


The *grade* will get you through college.
The *information* will get you through
life.

—Ken Weinraub, college student

---

### Tip #392

If you think it's going to be difficult to graduate, think about how difficult it will be to compete against someone who has graduated if you haven't.

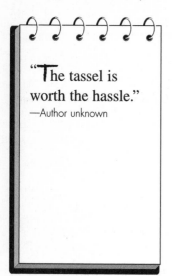

"The tassel is worth the hassle."
—Author unknown

### Tip #393

Remember: If Forrest Gump can graduate, so can you!

### Tip #394

Make sure you attend your graduation as a participant—not as a spectator.

### Tip #395

Once you get your degree, no one will ever be able to take it away from you. It's yours forever.

### Tip #396

If your goal is just to graduate, you're aiming too low.

## Tip #397

Here's a gauge to determine whether you'll graduate: If you play cards more than you study—you won't. If you play video games more than you study—you won't. If you watch TV more than you study—you won't.

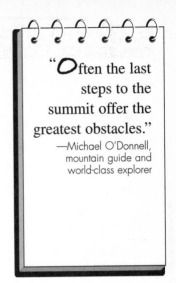

"*O*ften the last steps to the summit offer the greatest obstacles."
—Michael O'Donnell, mountain guide and world-class explorer

## Tip #398

If you want to graduate, make sure you don't major in minor things.

## Tip #399

Remember, getting through college is not a sprint; it's a marathon. And you'll get the best results if you're part of a relay team.

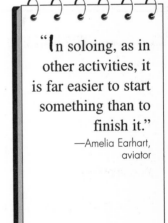

"*I*n soloing, as in other activities, it is far easier to start something than to finish it."
—Amelia Earhart, aviator

## Tip #400

The pain is temporary; the pride is forever.

## Tip #401

Your college degree will change your life FOREVER.

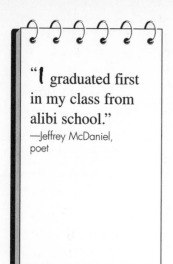

## Tip #402

Read *How to Have Fun Without Failing Out* at least two more times and keep it with your textbooks. If you've read this far and this book hasn't helped—check your pulse!

## Tip #403

You already have all the ingredients you need to be a successful college student. This book is your recipe. If you follow the advice on these pages—FAILURE IS IMPOSSIBLE.

---

### REALITY CHECK #4

*Any time you don't want to do something mentioned in this book, remember these six motivational words:*
**"Do you want fries with that?"**

---

## Tip #404

Here are fourteen words from Coach Oliver Gelston that'll change your life:

"Be at the right place,
at the right time,
and do the right thing."

## How to Have Fun Without Failing Out!

✓ Give your favorite graduates the world's greatest graduation present: Oh, the Places You'll Go *by Dr. Seuss.*

✓ Many alumni report that one of the most rewarding things they ever did was volunteer for a literacy program to help someone learn to read.

✓ After you graduate, keep in touch with your favorite professors and something amazing might happen—they might turn into friends! Want proof? Get the book Tuesdays with Morrie *by Mitch Albom (Random House, 2002)—also get a box of tissues.*

"A graduation ceremony is an event where the commencement speaker tells thousands of students dressed in identical caps and gowns that 'individuality' is the key to success."

—Robert Orben, comedy writer

## Chapter 9

---

**From:**     Rob Gilbert, Ph.D.

**To:**       Students

**Subject:**  Planning Your Career

The purpose of life is to discover your gifts. The meaning of life comes from giving your gifts away.

—Dr. David Viscott, psychiatrist

---

### Tip #405

Theologian Howard Thurman's advice on careers: "Don't ask what the world needs. Ask what makes you come alive, and go do it. Because what the world needs is people who have come alive."

### Tip #406

Of all the things you can discover in college, the most important is your passion.

### Tip #407

Take a tip from Jack Nicklaus, one of the greatest golfers of all time: "It's difficult to excel at something you don't truly enjoy."

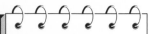

"The person who gets hired is not necessarily the one who can do that job best; but, the one who knows the most about how to get hired."
—Richard Bolles, career expert and author

### Tip #408

The absolute best book for finding or changing a career is *What Color Is Your Parachute 2007: A Practical Manual for Job-Hunters and Career-Changers* by Richard Nelson Bolles (Ten Speed Press, 2006). Check out the supplemental website www.JobHuntersBible.com.

## Tip #409

No one would buy a pair of shoes without trying them on, so why do so many graduates go into a profession without first "trying it on"? For example, if you want to be an accountant, do an internship or co-op in an accounting firm. Get a part-time job with an accountant. If nothing else, volunteer to work in the field.

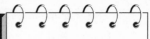

"**N**o one can fault you for being too formal. Sloppy appearance, you have no shot. Show respect for the process and the employer."

—John McCarthy, educator and professional speaker

## Tip #410

Never look for just a job. Always think in terms of a career.

## Tip #411

Your school's alumni association can help put you in touch with successful graduates from your major.

## Tip #412

All the strategies you need to know to become outrageously successful in any career can be found right on campus.

## Tip #413

Go to the career services office well before your senior year.

## Tip #414

Get an education, not just a degree, because twenty years from now, you will have a job that doesn't exist yet.

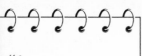

> "If you follow your bliss, doors will open for you that wouldn't have opened for anyone else."
> —Joseph Campbell, professor and writer

### Tip #415

When you don't know what you want to do for a career, think about how you would spend your time if you had all the money in the world.

### Tip #416

If you always need a boss, you'll always have a boss. The ultimate absolute essential is for you to **BYOB** (**B**e **Y**our **O**wn **B**oss). In other words, you have to get yourself to do what you have to do, when you have to do it, whether you like it or not . . . no matter what!

### Tip #417

Attend professional conferences and read professional journals in the field of your major.

### Tip #418

Write your resume *well* before you're going to need it because you're going to need it *well* before you think you will.

### Tip #419

If you *really* want to be a doctor, a lawyer, or a psychologist, the work to become one will be no problem.

### Tip #420

How you spend your four (or five) years in college will determine how you spend your next forty (or fifty) years after college.

### Tip #421

Become incredibly interested in the future because you're going to spend the rest of your life there.

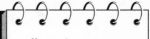

"When people are highly motivated, it's easy to accomplish the impossible. And when they're not, it's impossible to accomplish the easy."
—Bob Collins

## Interviewing

### Tip #422

Learn how to interview successfully. Practice interviewing. Out-interview the other candidates for the job.

### Tip #423

Before any job interview, review your answers to these questions:

Why should we hire you?
What is your greatest strength?
What is your greatest weakness?
What sets you apart from other applicants?

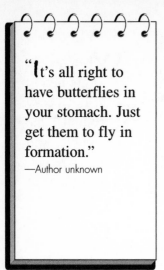

### Tip #424

When you interview, answer each question in fewer than sixty seconds.

### Tip #425

Do your research. Learn about the company, its history, and its personnel. If possible, also learn about the interviewer's professional background.

### Tip #426

Keep the jargon professional and never use strong language or swear.

### Tip #427

Many companies hire for attitude and train for skill.

### Tip #428

Wear a well-tailored suit to all job interviews. First impressions are very important.

## Tip #429

The ultimate goal of education: to learn how to learn on your own. "Give people a fish and they'll eat for a day. Teach people to fish and they'll eat for a lifetime."

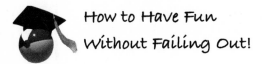

## How to Have Fun Without Failing Out!

✓ Keep a file or portfolio labeled "Stuff That Makes Me Look Great" and include:
- Letters of recommendation
- Letters of congratulations
- Thank-you notes
- Academic and athletic honors and awards
- Newsclips about your achievements
- Copies of programs, photos, or videos from events you performed in or organized

This will remind you of the star you are and serve to impress others when you're applying for scholarships, graduate school, or jobs.

✓ If you start thinking, "I don't have any time to have fun," read this book again!

# The Diploma

One day a middle-aged woman clutching a plastic bag close to her chest walked into a picture-framing store.

She looked at the manager behind the counter and said, "I have something in this bag that cost me over $150,000, but it's worth much more than that."

"May I see it?" asked the manager.

Carefully and with great pride, the woman unrolled her daughter's college diploma.

# ONE LAST THING . . .

This book cannot become successful unless you become successful. If there is any way I can help you, e-mail me at: sendmeastory@aol.com.

Also, if you have an idea or an item that could be added to *How to Have Fun Without Failing Out*, please e-mail it to me at the address above.

Thousands and thousands of students just like you have been motivated by my Success Hotline. Every morning since 1992, I have been recording three-minute motivational messages, which you can listen to 24/7/365. Call Success Hotline right now: (973) 743-4690.

Oh, one last thing . . .

I've given you my absolute best advice. The *good* news is that all the tips in this book have one thing in common: they work. The *bad* news is that they will only work if you work them. Therefore, here's my last tip:

## Tip #430

Reading these tips is not enough—you have to live them.